Richard Scarry's
First Little Learners Treasury

From 1 to 10

J-B Communications
Derrydale Books™
New York

Can you help
Miss Honey
count to ten?

Of course,
you can!

4

One

MARCHING BAGPIPER

TWO

FRIENDLY POLICEMEN

Three
BUSY ARTISTS

Four
SPEEDY MOTORBOATS

5

Five
FUNNY SAILORS

9

6

Six
COLORFUL KITES

Seven

FIRE ENGINES

Eight

LITTLE AIRPLANES

Nine

HAPPY MAIL CARRIERS

Ten

GREAT BIG GRUMPY GUARDS!

Colors

Lowly's apple car is red.

So is his sneaker.

Greenbug's tomato car is red.

Fire engines
are red.

Good for you!

23

Blue is the color of blueberries.

Blue is the color of the sea and of the sky.

24

Huckle Cat's
and Lowly's pajamas
are blue.

There goes a
blue racing car!

Father Bear's jacket
is blue, too.

Oh dear!

Do you know what Bananas Gorilla's favorite color is? Why, yellow, of course!

Yellow is the color of Bananas' Bananamobile...

... and of banana peels, too.

26

A school bus is yellow.

Lemons are yellow...

... and cheese cars are yellow, too!

Blue mixed with yellow makes green.

Pickles are green.

So is the pickle truck.

Pig Won't's overalls are green.

Tree leaves are green.

Cabbage cars are green, greenbugs, too!

White mixed with red makes pink.

Rabbit noses are pink.

Hilda's dress is pink.   So are Lowly's roses.

Pink is the color of Mistress Mouse's repair truck.

Strawberry ice cream is pink.

...and it tastes delicious!

BLACK

Black is the color of tires.

Coal is black.

WHITE

Snowflakes
are white.

Ambulances are white.

Ice-cream trucks, too!

33

White mixed with black makes gray.

Huckle's trousers
are gray.

So is cement.

Yellow, red and blue, when mixed together...

... make brown.

Mud is brown.

It's sticky, too!

Red mixed with blue makes purple.

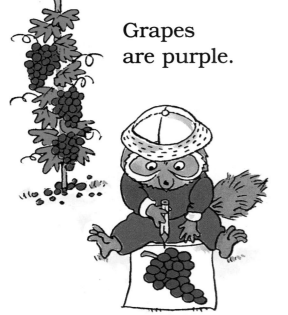

Grapes
are purple.

Violets
are purple.

Red mixed with yellow makes orange.

Oranges
are orange.

Orange juice, too!

37

Shapes and Opposites

SHANES

This is a triangle.

A pennant has the shape of a triangle.

This is a square.

A checkerboard has the shape of a square.

This is a circle.

A full moon has the shape of a circle...

... so do buttons!

This is a rectangle.

This is, too!

Books have the shape of a rectangle.

This is a diamond.

This shape is a star.

Kites are diamond-shaped.

Good for you, Freddie!

LINES

This line is curved.

This line is straight.

Jump ropes have curved lines.

A ruler has a straight line.

Spaghetti noodles have squiggly lines.

Willy is drawing a zig-zag line.

crossed lines

Some lines are thin...

... others are thick.

Lines that go the same direction
are parallel lines.

Lined paper
has parallel lines.

A line of dashes is a broken line.

Mr. Paint Pig paints a broken line
on the street.

A line of dots is a dotted line.

(You can write your name on this dotted line.)

43

WHICH WAY?

above

The airplane flies
above the boat.

between

The submarine
goes under the boat.

below

Dad is
ahead.

Son is
behind him.

right-side up

upside-down

Tommy pulls
to the left.

Timmy pulls
to the right.

44

going over

going around

going under

Arthur has placed
his lunchbox beside him.
He sits beside it.

Mr. Frumble drives
backward.

Mr. Frumble
drives forward.

My, he doesn't drive very well, does he?

45

HIGH AND LOW

This bug
is high up.

This plane
is going
up.

This bug
is low down.

This plane
is going
down.

at the
top

at the
bottom

This bear
is down.

This bear
is up.

46

The mouse is small.

BIG AND SMALL

The elephant is big.

This piggy is fat.

Lowly is thin.

Hilda is heavy.

Dandelion seeds are light.

47

AMOUNTS

The bakers have lots of cupcakes.

Lowly eats one.

Thank you, bakers!

The children's breakfast bowls are full.

When they have finished eating, the bowls are empty.

They bring their bowls back to the kitchen. Aren't they helpful!

A bus carries many people.

A pencil car carries just a couple.

Hilda is eating
all the cookies.

Lowly
has none.

Hey!
You should share!

OPPOSITES

front   back

good boys

bad boys

Mr. Rabbit stays dry.   Mr. Frumble gets wet.

These pupils are noisy.

Huckle is quiet.
He is reading.

Oops!
The bridge is too
narrow!
The car is too
wide!

Albert's barge goes slowly.

clean pig   dirty pig

You need a bath!

Roger's plane goes fast.

A wooden stool is hard.

A pillow is soft.

It's hot!

It's cold!

Huckle and Lowly are laughing.

Willy is crying.

Hey! Be a good sport!

54

Mr. Frumble came too early
to the dentist.
He must wait his turn.

Mr. Frumble was too late at the bus stop.

Now he must
wait for the
next bus.

Sophie is awake.

Arthur is
sleeping.

So please be quiet,
Sophie!

55

This is Me

WHAT A WONDERFUL PERSON I AM !

I can look.

I can stand.

I can walk.

I can run.

I can jump.

Sometimes I fall.

Ouch!

Be brave!

And sometimes I cry if I'm hurt.

LOOK WHAT I CAN DO.

I can listen.

I can talk.

I can see.

I can smell.

I can touch.

I can eat. Yum!

And when I sleep,
I have nice
dreams.

I can wash myself.

comb

I'M NO LONGER A BABY.

brush

I can comb myself.

soap

I can take a bath
by myself.

towel

water

I can brush my teeth.

toothpaste

I always put my things away neatly.
Mommy likes that.

Mommy has taught
me to sew on buttons...

... and how to make
my bed all by myself!

I have a head.

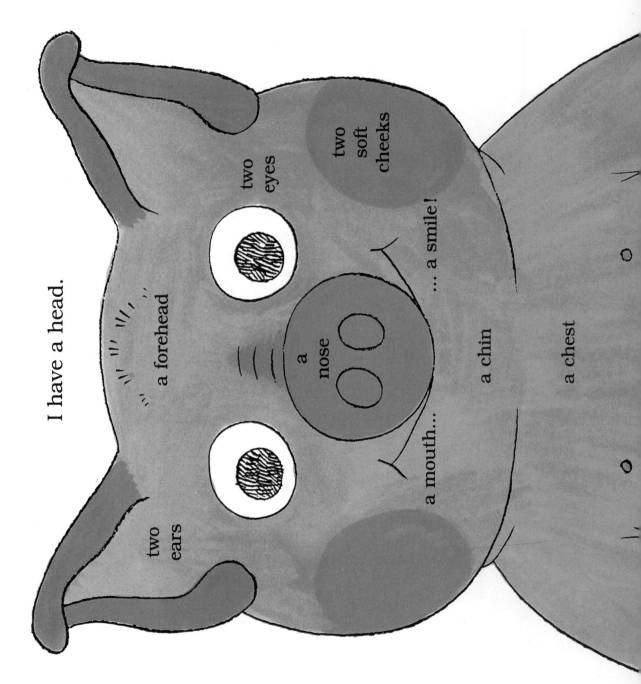

two ears

a forehead

two eyes

two soft cheeks

a nose

a mouth...

...a smile!

a chin

a chest

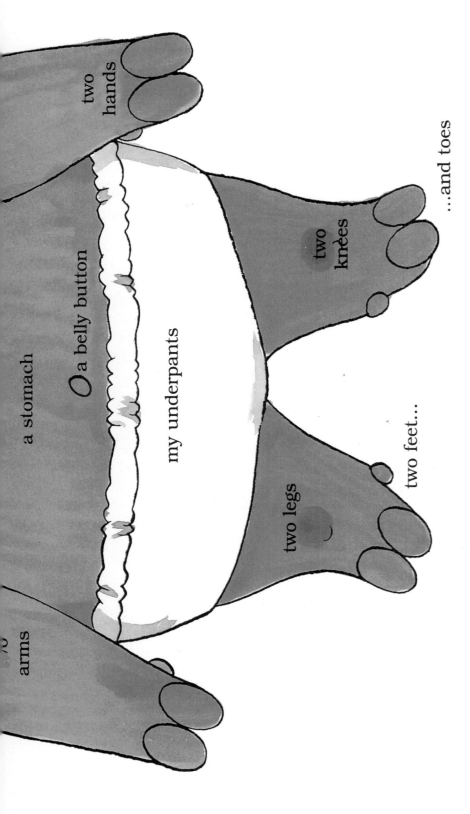

two hands

...and toes

a stomach

a belly button

two knees

my underpants

two feet...

two legs

arms

**THIS IS ME
FROM THE FRONT.**

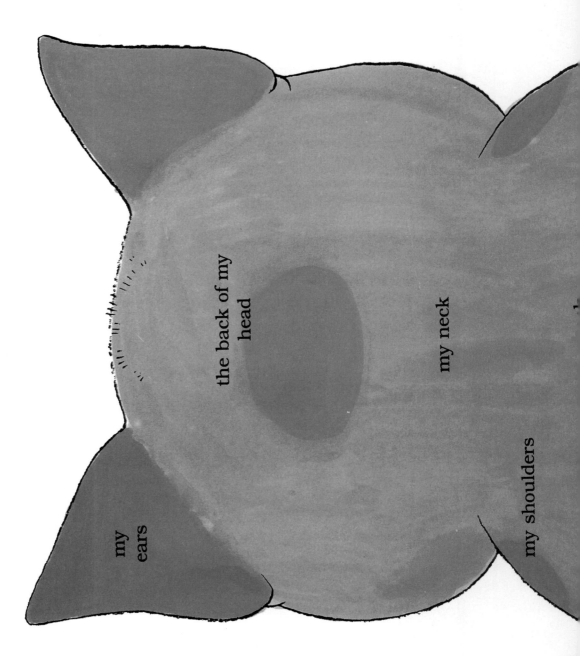

my ears

the back of my head

my neck

my shoulders

66

my hands

my feet...
...and toes.

my curly
tail

my waist

my ankle

my bottom

an elbow

my wrist

THIS IS ME
FROM BEHIND.

67

LOOK AT ALL MY CLOTHES.

shirt

blazer

overcoat

jacket

overalls

sweater

vest

undershirt

underpants

sneakers

belt

socks

wrist watch

blue jeans

dress

skirt

blouse

bonnet

purse

tights

handbag

hair comb

sunhat

headband

necklace

earrings

ring

I CAN
DRESS MYSELF.

closet

Hey! That's no way to put
on your shorts!

suspenders

coat hanger

socks

cap

bathrobe

70

When I go to
a party, I get
dressed up.

bow tie

handkerchief

necktie

I bring flowers
as a gift.

slippers

sandals

pajamas

nightie

When I go to bed at night,
this is what I wear.

I DRESS DIFFERENTLY
FOR ALL KINDS OF WEATHER.

In winter, I dress for the cold.

earmuffs

mittens

wool hat

gloves

ski jacket

snowsuit

my sled

scarf

ice skates

When it rains, I dress to keep dry.

rainhat

umbrella

raincoat

boots

puddle

rubbers

In summer, at the beach, this is what I wear :

sunhat

sunglasses

swimsuit

This is My House

It has
a roof.

It has windows.

It has a
backdoor.

76

It has
a chimney.

THIS IS MY HOUSE.

This is my angry
brother.

It has
a terrace.

It has a front door.

It has a
porch.

lantern

our
mailbox

THIS IS THE KITCHEN.

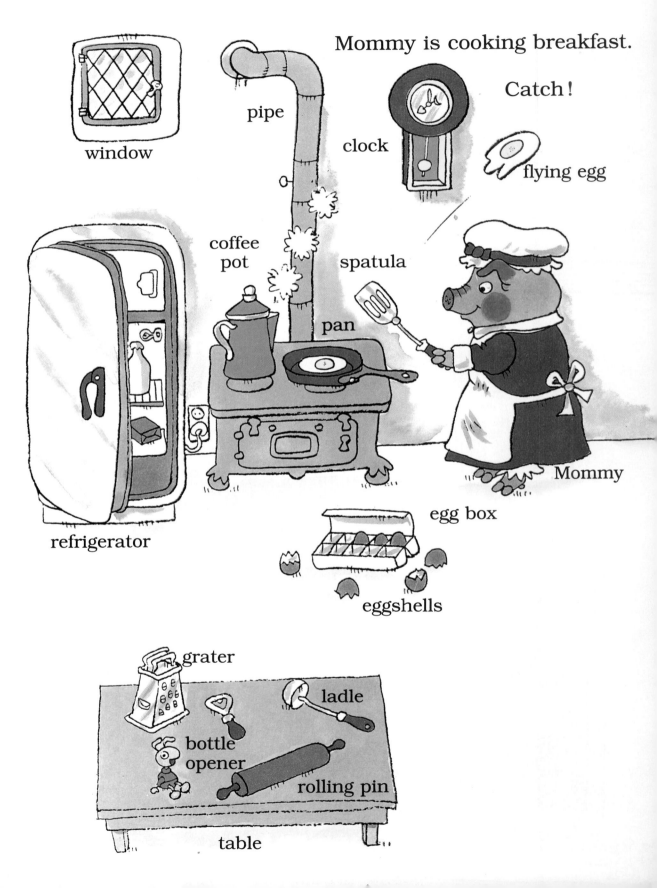

window

pipe

Mommy is cooking breakfast.

Catch!

clock

flying egg

coffee pot

spatula

pan

refrigerator

Mommy

egg box

eggshells

grater

ladle

bottle opener

rolling pin

table

whisk

pot

pan

handrail

pitcher

flying toast

teapot

creamer

toaster

staircase

plate

fork

knife

glass

salt and pepper

chair

stool

spoon

tablecloth

jam

THIS IS THE LIVING ROOM.

Daddy is going to work.
Don't be late!

window

curtain rod

priceless
painting

curtains

lamp

candle

candlestick

armchair

antenna

chess game

table

television
set

books

rug

another priceless painting

front door

paintbrush
and
paintbucket

keys

Daddy

steps

THIS IS THE BEDROOM.

piggy bank

lamp

chest of
drawers

sleepy
brother

blanket

stairwell

slippers

toy chest

pillow

noisy
sister

closet

window

bedside
table

noisy
brother

rug

unmade bed

Hey! Who forgot
to make his bed?

83

THIS IS THE BATHROOM.

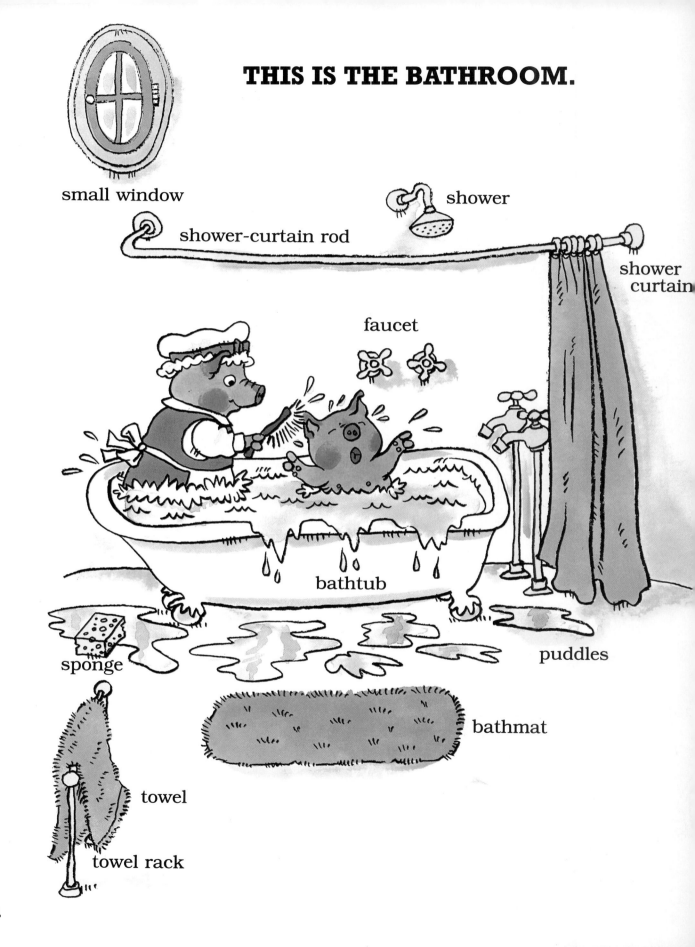

small window

shower

shower-curtain rod

shower
curtain

faucet

bathtub

sponge

puddles

bathmat

towel

towel rack

lights

cabinet

medicine cabinet

faucet

sink

soap

toothbrush

toilet paper

towel

be of toothpaste

waste-basket

comb

brush

toilet

toilet brush

table

THE BASEMENT IS BENEATH THE HOUSE.

lamp

light switch

handrail

fuse box

Never, never touch!

stairway

electric plug

bucket

mat

mop

brush

washing machine

laundry basket

detergent

radio

vase of flowers

THIS IS MOMMY'S STUDY.

window

bookcase

Hello!

typewriter

curtains

writing paper

a ringing telephone

chair

dictionary

fire extinguisher

water heater

furnace

THE ATTIC IS UNDER THE ROOF.

carpenter

hammer

ladder

nail

shingles

new shingles

dusty attic

old scooter

A mason building the chimney.

trowel

bricks

roof

old lamp

old sewing machine

old kite

old roller skates

old wheel

gutter

89

WHERE DO YOU LIVE?
WHERE WOULD YOU LIKE TO LIVE?

In a cozy wooden chalet?

In an igloo made of ice?

water tower

taxi

In a tall apartment house?

laundry

In a houseboat?

thatched roof

In a cottage?

rope ladder

In a tree house?

In a wood-frame house?

garage

91

Cars and Trucks

DIFFERENT PEOPLE, DIFFERENT CARS

Mr. Paint Pig
needs a truck with
lots of space to
carry paint and
brushes.

mouse in
a racing car

The Cat family likes to
drive in an open
four-seat convertible.

mouse in a pencil car

Sergeant Murphy drives
a bright red motorcycle.

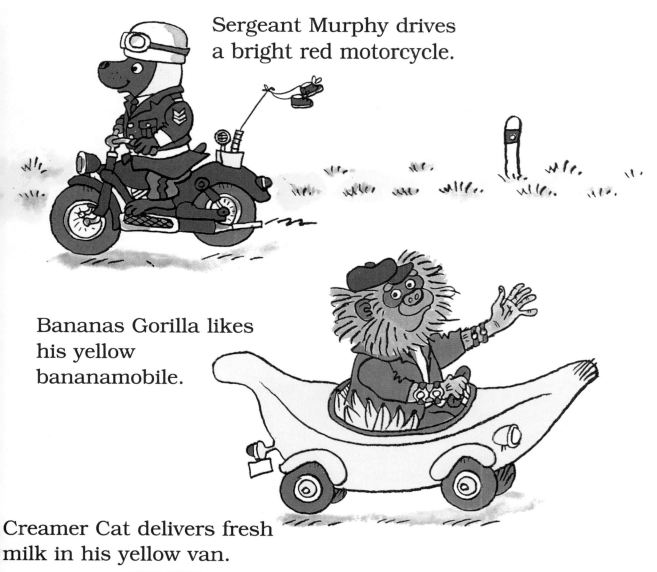

Bananas Gorilla likes
his yellow
bananamobile.

Creamer Cat delivers fresh
milk in his yellow van.

three bugs in
a green leaf car

flying pickles

dashing vintage roadster

Postman Pig picks up mail
in his mail van.

mailbox

great big tractor-trailer pickle truck

The Pig family
drives in a
station wagon.

Lowly Worm always
drives his apple car.

Harry Hyena
on roller skates

AT THE GARAGE

Greasy George's garage is a busy place for cars to be repaired, washed, and filled-up with gasoline.

Greasy George

A car having a bath.

happy mechanic

98

Gasoline is delivered to Greasy George's garage in this tank truck.

delivery man

underground gas tank

gas pump

Mother Cat's car gets a full tank of gasoline, and a clean windshield.

CARS AND TRUCKS
FOR BUSY HELPERS

siren radio

The policeman needs a speedy car to get quickly
where he is needed.

white ambulance
to carry patients
to the hospital

red fire trucks to race swiftly to a fire

tow trucks for repairmen...

... and for
repair women

jingling bells

There is an ice-cream truck

IN THE STREET

Here is a TV truck

Here comes the garbage truck,
picking up
garbage.

garbage can

There goes the
street sweeper,
cleaning the street.

Here is an Army car.

There goes a scooter...

... and there is
Mr. Frumble in
his pickle car.

Mind your
hat,
Mr. Frumble!

BUSY MACHINES

Here is a bucket scoop, digging a ditch.

the surveyor's plan

a marker string

Earmuffs protect against the noise.

A compressor compresses air for the jack-hammer

a detour sign

The jack-hammer digs up the pavement.

cone

104

Here is a crane,
laying a pipe.

crane
operator

driver

Here are two
busy workers.

Hey! Stop
chatting!

a jeep

105

steam-shovel
dumping rocks

tractor
dumping earth

bugdozer

an all-terrain
buggy

dump cart
carrying earth

106

dump truck
not watching
where it dumps

bulldozer
pushing earth

Here is the school bus,
carrying children to school.

WHICH CAR WOULD YOU LIKE TO DRIVE?

brooms

TV antenna

sun roof

The Pigs' camping car?

Mr. Fixit's hammer car?

mustard

Wilbur Rabbit's
hot dog car?

108

Tommy's taxi?

Captain Salty's
boat car?

A bug car?

Sprout Goat's
tractor?

Or Dingo Dog's
sports car?

Drive carefully!